Internet DOs & DON'Ts

Don't Share Your Plans Online

Shannon Miller

D1607169

PowerKiDS press.

New York

Published in 2014 by The Rosen Publishing Group, Inc.
29 East 21st Street, New York, NY 10010

First Edition

Editor: Jennifer Way
Book Design: Andrew Povolny

Photo Credits: Cover JGI Jamie Grill/Blend Images/Getty Images; p. 5 LWA/Dann Tardif/Blend Images/Getty Images; p. 7 Edward Lara/Shutterstock.com; p. 9 Brand X Images/Thinkstock; p. 11 Fotokostic/Shutterstock.com; p. 13 Andersen Ross/Blend Images/Getty Images; p. 15 Lars Trangius/Getty Images; p. 17 Wesley Hitt/Photographer's Choice/Getty Images; p. 19 John Giustina/The Image Bank/Getty Images; p. 21 Rob Marmion/Shutterstock.com; p. 23 Thomas Barwick/Photographer's Choice RF/Getty Images.

Library of Congress Cataloging-in-Publication Data
Miller, Shannon.
  Don't share your plans online / by Shannon Miller. — First Edition.
      pages cm. — (Internet dos & don'ts)
  Includes index.
  ISBN 978-1-4777-0754-8 (library binding) — ISBN 978-1-4777-1560-4 (pbk.) —
  ISBN 978-1-4777-1561-1 (6-pack)
  1. Internet—Safety measures. 2. Internet and children. I. Title.
  HQ784.I58M5495 2014
  025.04'0289—dc23
                                        2012050005

Manufactured in the United States of America

CPSIA Compliance Information: Batch #S13PK4: For Further Information contact Rosen Publishing, New York, New York at 1-800-237-9932

Contents

Do you play games online? Do you go online at school? You must use the **Internet** safely. This book will help you stay safe online.

Don't share your plans online! Plans are what you are going to do. Some plans are things you do every day.

The time you leave for school is a plan. The time you go home is a plan. How you go to and from school is a plan.

Some plans do not happen every day. They may be fun things you do. Playing with a friend is a plan. Going to a party is a plan.

A **stranger** may ask about your plans online. Strangers are people you do not know. Do not share your plans!

A stranger who knows your plans could follow you. He could find your home. That is scary. That is why you must not share your plans.

15

Tell an adult if a stranger bothers you. Tell an adult if you shared your plans. Ask for help. She will not be angry.

A trusted adult may be a teacher. He may be a coach or a parent. He wants you to be safe. He can help you.

An adult can find safe **websites**. Some are just for kids. Ask an adult to **bookmark** them. That makes them easy to find.

Now you know why it is not safe to share your plans. Never share your plans online. Never share your plans with strangers. Those are big Internet don'ts.

WORDS TO KNOW

bookmark (BOOK-mark) Saving a website's address in the browser.

Internet (IN-ter-net) A network that connects computers around the world. The Internet provides facts and information.

stranger (STRAYN-jer) A person you do not know.

website (WEB-syt) A place on the Internet.

INDEX

WEBSITES

Due to the changing nature of Internet links, PowerKids Press has developed an online list of websites related to the subject of this book. This site is updated regularly. Please use this link to access the list:
www.powerkidslinks.com/idd/plans/